First-Year Law Student

Bar Exam

& High-Grade Answers

October 2016

MARY T. PARDINEK

With Permission from the State Bar of California

October 2016 California BAR EXAM with ANSWERS for 1st Year Law Students

All rights reserved.

ISBN-13:
978-1976144196

ISBN-10:
1976144191

DEDICATION

Despite the dread and upset from my education in the University of Hard Knocks, good results did prevail. This book is one. Publication of it is to assist any 1st year law student with the resources and tools I wish I had when needed. Best Wishes to you in your scholastic studies and all future endeavors.

October 2016 California BAR EXAM with ANSWERS for 1st Year Law Students

CONTENTS

	Acknowledgments	7
1	Introduction and Essay Bar Exam Instructions	9
2	QUESTION 1	Pg #13
3	QUESTION 1: SELECTED ANSWER A	Pg #15
4	QUESTION 1: SELECTED ANSWER B	Pg #27
5	QUESTION 2	Pg #37
6	QUESTION 2: SELECTED ANSWER A	Pg #39
7	QUESTION 2: SELECTED ANSWER B	Pg #47

October 2016 California BAR EXAM with ANSWERS for 1st Year Law Students

8	QUESTION 3		Pg #53
9	QUESTION SELECTED ANSWER A	3:	Pg #55
10	QUESTION SELECTED ANSWER B	3:	Pg #61
11	QUESTION 4		Pg #67
12	QUESTION SELECTED ANSWER A	4:	Pg #69
13	QUESTION SELECTED ANSWER B	4:	Pg #79

ACKNOWLEDGMENTS

Passing a State Bar exam is a big deal for applicants. Many books assist. However, studying actual exams and correct answers is likely best. This book's contents show why other have passed. It includes a State Bar of California essay exam, with high-grade answers. Such a valuable study aid should assist any first-year law student. This excellent resource demonstrates proper applications of required terminology for understanding Contracts, Criminal Law, and Torts.

Attribution given to the State Bar of California for permission to publish this special resource. Thank you!

California First-Year Law Students' Examination

Essay Questions and Selected Answers

October 2016

INTRODUCTION

This publication contains the four essay questions from the October 2016 California First-Year Law Students' Examination and two selected answers for each question.

The answers were assigned high grades and were written by applicants who passed the examination. The answers were produced as submitted by the applicant, except that minor corrections in spelling and punctuation were made for ease in reading. They are reproduced here with the consent of the authors.

Question Number	Subject
1.	Criminal Law
2.	Contracts
3.	Torts
4.	Contracts

October 2016 California BAR EXAM with ANSWERS for 1st Year Law Students

INSTRUCTIONS

California First-Year Law Students' Examination

October 2016
ESSAY QUESTIONS

Answer all 4 questions.

Your answer should demonstrate your ability to analyze the facts in the question, to tell the difference between material facts and immaterial facts, and to discern the points of law and fact upon which the case turns. Your answer should show that you know and understand the pertinent principles and theories of law, their qualifications and limitations, and their relationships to each other.

Your answer should evidence your ability to apply the law to the given facts and to reason in a logical, lawyer-like manner from the premises you adopt to a sound conclusion. Do not merely show that you remember legal principles. Instead, try to demonstrate your proficiency in using and applying them.

If your answer contains only a statement of your conclusions, you will receive little credit. State fully the reasons that support your conclusions, and discuss all points thoroughly.

Your answer should be complete, but you should not volunteer information or discuss legal doctrines that are not pertinent to the solution of the problem.

You should answer according to legal theories and principles of general application.

QUESTION 1

Al and Beth were sitting in Al's apartment, playing video games and drinking beer. After finishing the last beer, Al said to Beth, "I need another beer. Can you lend me some money and drive me to the store?"

Beth responded, "I can drive you to the store, but I don't have any money."

Al laughed and said, "I have an idea for how to get some beer without paying for it. Drive me to the store and park behind it near the emergency exit."

Beth drove Al to the Friendly Market and waited in the car near the emergency exit. Al entered the store, picked up a six-pack of beer, and began walking toward the emergency exit.

Carla, a security guard, was watching Al. As Al approached the exit, Carla shouted, "Stop, thief!" Al put the beer on the floor and ran out through the emergency exit.

For a few seconds, Carla considered what to do. Then she ran after Al. In the alley behind the store, she shouted, "Stop or I'll shoot!" When Al did not stop, Carla fired a warning shot. When Al kept running, Carla took careful aim, shot, and missed. As Al was about to run around a corner, Carla paused, took careful aim, shot again, and killed him.

1. Can it be reasonably argued that Beth is guilty of a. Theft? Discuss. b. Robbery? Discuss. c. Murder? Discuss.

2. Can it be reasonably argued that Carla is guilty of murder and, if so, what defense(s) can she raise? Discuss.

QUESTION 1: SELECTED ANSWER A

1. STATE v. BETH

Conspiracy

A conspiracy is an agreement between two or more persons to commit an unlawful act; under a majority jurisdiction, an overt act is required.

Beth will contend that there was no meeting of the minds between her and Al to commit an unlawful act, as when Al asked her for money she told him that she didn't have any money.

The state will argue that when Al told Beth that he "had an idea for how to get some beer without paying for it" and directed her to "drive me to the store and park behind it near the emergency exit," that her voluntary act in driving

Al to the Friendly Market constituted her agreement. It can be reasoned from Al's statement to Beth that she knew how Al planned to get beer without paying for it which meant that he intended to commit an unlawful act, namely to steal the beer from the store. Thus, Beth's conduct was the assent to the plan of stealing the beer. The overt act element was satisfied when Beth drove Al to the Friendly Market for Al to effectuate the plan.

Therefore, Beth will be charged with conspiracy.

Pinkerton's Rule

A co-conspirator will be liable for all crimes committed by the other conspirators that are foreseeable and in furtherance of the target crime.
Because Beth is a co-conspirator with Al, she will be charged with larceny, the intended crime, as discussed infra, and all other foreseeable crimes committed by Al.

Principal in the Second

Under common law, a principal in the second is one who actively aids and abets in the commission of the crime and is actually and constructively present at the time of the commission of the crime.

Beth drove Al to the Friendly Market and waited in the car near the emergency exit, and thus, she actively provided her assistance to aid Al to steal the beer. Al is the perpetrator and principal in the first. Because Beth is actually present out at the back of the Friendly Market, she will be deemed a principal in the second under common law.

Therefore, Beth is a principal in the second degree.

Accomplice Liability

Modernly, the designation of all who aid and assist in the commission of the crime is known as an accomplice. An accomplice is one who actively aids and assists in the commission of a crime.

Because Beth knew and was aware of how Al was going to obtain the beer without paying for it, and because thereafter, she voluntarily drove Al to the store for him to effectuate his plan, she intended for Al to steal the beer by actively aiding him to steal the beer.

Therefore, Beth is an accomplice and will be liable for all crimes that are foreseeable during the commission of the target crime.

1a. Theft - Larceny

Larceny is the trespassory taking and carrying away the personal property of another with the intent to permanently deprive the owner thereof.

Upon arrival at the Friendly Market, Al entered the store, picked up a six-pack of beer and began walking toward the emergency exit. This constitutes a trespassory taking because he intended on taking it without paying for it, and thus did not have the owner's consent to take it.

Furthermore, in order for him to walk toward the emergency exit with the beer, he had to pick up the beer and carry it away from where he found it; thus the element of carrying away has been satisfied. Lastly, as Al planned that Beth would drive him to the store where he would "get some beer without paying for it," he had the intent to permanently deprive the owner of the beer at the time he entered the store and took the beer.

Therefore, Beth will be charged with larceny.

1b. Robbery

Robbery is the trespassory taking and carrying away the personal property of another with the intent to permanently deprive the owner thereof by force, fear or intimidation.

As discussed above, the elements of larceny are satisfied and thus larceny has been committed. The facts indicate that Al entered the Friendly Market without incident, and proceeded to pick up a six-pack of beer and began walking toward the emergency exit. It was only after he began walking toward the emergency exit that Carla realized that Al had taken the beer and was going to leave the store without paying for it. In fact, when Carla shouted "Stop, thief," Al put the beer on the floor and ran out.

Thus, Beth will argue that because Al took the beer without any force, fear or intimidation, a robbery was not committed.

Therefore, Beth will not be charged with robbery.

1c. Murder

Homicide

A homicide is an unlawful killing of a human being by another.

When Al ran from the store, Carla, who was a security guard at the Friendly Market, took chase and shot and killed Al. The killing was unlawful as it could be ascertained from the facts that Al died prematurely.

Therefore, there is a homicide of Al.

Actual Cause

But for Beth driving Al to the Friendly Market, and but for Carla shooting Al in hot pursuit, Al would not have died.

Therefore, Beth is the actual cause of Al's death.

Proximate Cause

Beth will contend that Carla shooting Al is an intervening act that breaks the chain of causation to hold her liable for Al's death.
However, the state will assert that it is foreseeable that if you conspire to steal from a grocery store, thus committing an unlawful act, that someone is bound to be injured. Furthermore, it is foreseeable that the store would be attended by a security guard to prevent theft. Thus, although Carla may have intervened when she shot and killed Al, her actions were foreseeable, and Al's death is foreseeable.

Therefore, Beth is the proximate cause of Al's death.

Murder

Murder is the unlawful killing of another with malice aforethought.

Malice Aforethought

Malice may be found: (1) if defendant had the intent to kill; (2) if defendant had the intent to cause great bodily harm; (3) if defendant acted with reckless and unjustifiable risk to human life (depraved heart); or (4) through the application of the felony murder rule.

Intent to Kill or Cause Great Bodily Harm

Because Al was the co-conspirator with Beth, and because Al was the victim that died, it cannot be imputed upon Beth Carla's intent to kill or cause great bodily harm, if she expressed such intent.

Therefore, malice will not be established through intent to kill or cause great bodily harm.

Depraved Heart

The state will argue that Beth driving Al to the store to steal beer as wanton and reckless because stealing from a store could produce the likely result that someone, including Al, could be killed or seriously harmed.
Beth will contend that her actions were not wanton or reckless under the circumstances as all she did was provide transportation for Al to get to the Friendly Market. Furthermore, Al intended to steal a six-pack of beer, which such misdemeanor would not necessarily cause death or great bodily harm. Thus, if anything her conduct may be identified as being negligent.

Therefore, the state will not find malice by depraved heart.

Felony Murder Rule

Felony murder will be applied if the death occurred during the commission of an inherently dangerous felony.

The inherently dangerous felonies for which felony murder would be applied are: burglary, arson, robbery, mayhem, kidnapping, sodomy and sexual molestation. Because Al died as a result of a larceny, which is not one of the named inherently dangerous felonies, as opposed to robbery, as discussed supra, felony murder will not apply.

Therefore, the state will not find malice through the felony murder rule.

First-Degree Murder

First-degree murder is if the defendant commissioned the killing with the intent to kill with premeditation and deliberation, the killing occurred as a result of the defendant lying in wait, by poison, bomb or torture.

Because the state will fail to establish malice aforethought, there is no murder, and thus there is no application of first-degree murder.

Involuntary Manslaughter

Involuntary manslaughter is when the killing was unintended and occurred during the commission of a misdemeanor or as a result of defendant's criminal negligence.

Because the state will fail to find murder as to Beth, the state will look to charge Beth with involuntary manslaughter of Al. Since Beth provided active assistance to Al for Al to effectuate his plan to steal beer, her conduct was criminally negligent because although Al's death may have been unintended, she should have known that helping someone steal would result in a bad outcome such as death.

Therefore, Beth will be charged with involuntary manslaughter.

2. STATE v. CARLA

Homicide

As defined and discussed supra.

Actual Cause

But for Carla shooting Al, Al would not have died.

Therefore, Carla is the actual cause of Al's death.

Proximate Cause

Carla taking aim and shooting Al is a direct cause to Al's death.

Therefore, Carla is the proximate cause of Al's death.

Murder

As defined supra.

<u>Intent to Kill or Cause Great Bodily Harm</u>

The state will contend that Carla had the intent to kill Al when she ran after Al after Al had already put the six-pack of beer on the floor of the store, and she took careful aim and shot and killed Al. In order for Carla to stop and take careful aim at Al with the gun, she must have had the desire that pulling the trigger would result in the bullet striking and killing Al. Even if the bullet from her gun did not kill Al, Carla had the minimum desire to cause Al great bodily harm.

Therefore, the state will be able to establish malice by intent to kill or cause great bodily harm.

Depraved Heart

The state will claim that Carla's conduct was wanton and reckless because Al had already put the beer on the floor and ran out through the emergency exit. As Al ran away from the store, Carla ran after him and fired a warning shot. Furthermore, when Al kept running, Carla took careful aim, shot and missed Al, but then thereafter paused and took careful aim and shot again while Al was rounding the corner of the alley. Carla acted with a total disregard and her actions were unjustifiable insofar as she did not consider that the bullets from her gun could have harmed or killed bystanders.

Therefore, Carla was wanton and reckless.

First-Degree Murder

As defined above.

The state will argue that not only did Carla have the requisite intent to kill, the second time she took careful aim and shot again which killed Al, she acted with premeditation and deliberation because she had paused before taking the second shot at Al.

However, Carla will argue that she was chasing Al in hot pursuit and thus, she did not have the time to deliberate or premeditate before firing the shot at Al.

Therefore, Carla will not most likely not be charged with first-degree murder.

Second-Degree Murder

Second-degree murder is all other murders not first degree.

Since the state will be unable to prove its case against Carla for first-degree murder, Carla will be charged with second-degree murder.

Voluntary Manslaughter

Voluntary manslaughter is a killing that would be otherwise be murder but was committed with adequate provocation.

Carla will assert that she was adequately provoked to shoot Al because she was protecting the property of her employer. However, the state will contend that Carla did not act reasonably under the circumstances because Al, the assailant, had already put the beer on the floor of the store, and ran away from the store without the beer. Carla could have stopped right then and there as there was no need to chase Al. Thus, there was not adequate provocation.

Therefore, Carla's second-degree murder charge will not mitigate to voluntary manslaughter unless Carla has a viable defense.

Crime Prevention

A defendant is privileged to use reasonable deadly force to prevent a felony from occurring. A defendant may only use reasonable non-deadly force to prevent a misdemeanor.

Carla will assert that she was privileged in shooting Al as she was trying to prevent a crime from occurring.

However, the state will contend that because Al had already ran from the store without the beer, and that he was running away from Carla in the alley, that Carla did not act reasonably when she took careful aim and shot at Al. It was even more unreasonable of her to pause and take careful aim and shot again at Al when he was about to round the corner, as he was no longer on the premises.

Therefore, Carla's actions were not justified under the circumstances.

Therefore, crime prevention will not be a viable defense for Carla.

QUESTION 1: SELECTED ANSWER B

CAN IT BE REASONABLY ARGUED THAT BETH IS GUILTY OF THEFT, ROBBERY, AND MURDER?

In order for Beth to be guilty of theft, robbery and murder, she must have committed the acts herself, through an agent or through accomplice liability.

ACCOMPLICE LIABILITY
Accomplice liability establishes that any person that aids and abets another in the commission of a crime will be held vicariously liable for that crime and any foreseeable consequence of that crime.

Here, Beth aided and abetted Al because she drove him to the store. Here, Al solicited (asked) Beth for money and a drive to the store. When Beth did not have any money, she conspired (agreed) with Al to drive him to the store.

Here, Beth also aided and abetted because she knew Al had a plan to get beer without any money and she continued with provided assistance by waiting while Al went into the store. Beth knew that Al didn't have any money because he had already asked for money and Beth didn't have any to provide. Beth knew that when Al went into the store that he would most likely steal the beer because he told her I have an idea and gave her instructions to park in the back near the emergency exit.

Therefore, Beth can be held as an accomplice for the crimes of theft, robbery and murder if Al is guilty of those crimes.

LARCENY
Larceny is a trespassory taking and carry away the tangible personal property of another with the intent to permanently deprive.

Here, it can be argued that the taking wasn't trespassory because Friendly Market is a market open to the public for anyone to go in and do shopping. However, Al entered the store with the intent to get more beer when he knew he didn't have the money to pay for anything. When he picked up the beer, he had a plan to exit the store through the emergency exit because he had Beth waiting for him with the car to make a quick escape. Therefore, there is a trespassory taking. The property is of another because it is the lawful possession of Friendly Market until Al legally purchased the beer. Therefore, the property was of another. Al had the intent to permanently deprive because he had an escape plan to take the beer and later drink it.

Even though Al put the beer on the floor and left the store without the product, moving the tangible property slightly is all that counts. When Al picked up the beer and had the intent to permanently deprive, he committed a larceny.

Because Al could be guilty of larceny, Beth will also be guilty of the theft because she aided and abetted Al in the commission of the crime.

Therefore, Beth will be guilty of theft.

ROBBERY
Robbery is a larceny with immediate force or threat of force to accomplish the taking. Larceny would merge into robbery if the crime of robbery was completed.

Larceny was defined supra. The question here is whether or not Al committed the larceny with any force or threat of force. Here, it doesn't appear that there is any force because Al entered the store and picked up the beer and began walking toward the emergency exit. Al didn't use any force to pick it up.

Therefore, since Al would not be guilty of robbery, Beth would not have any accomplice liability for a robbery.

MURDER
In order to determine if Beth is guilty of murder, it must be established that Beth was involved with the events that lead to Al's death. Murder is a homicide committed with malice aforethought.

HOMICIDE
Homicide is the killing of a human being by the defendant's acts.

Here, there was a killing because Al is dead.

CAUSATION
The defendant must be the actual and proximate cause of the victim's death in order to be guilty of a homicide.

Here, Beth did not shoot Al and could only be guilty of the murder through vicarious liability if the murder occurred during the commission of an inherently dangerous felony. If Beth was found to be a co-felon, then the causation element would be established through vicarious liability.

Therefore, there is a homicide.

MALICE AFORETHOUGHT
Malice aforethought can be established through intent to kill/murder, intent to cause serious bodily injury, or through a killing that occurred during the commission of an inherently dangerous felony. It is clear from the facts that intent to kill/murder and intent to cause serious bodily injury are not at issue here.

WANTON CONDUCT
Wanton conduct is a death that occurred through extreme reckless disregard for human life.

Here, it may be argued that because Beth knew that Al didn't have any money to purchase the beer that he may do something illegal in order to obtain the beer.

However, Beth only provided assistance by driving Al to the store and waiting in the car. Beth didn't have any conduct that would elicit extreme disregard for human life because she wasn't actively involved with Al's idea to get beer without money.

Therefore, wanton conduct cannot be found.

FELONY MURDER RULE
Felony murder rule establishes vicarious liability for any death that occurs during the commission of an inherently dangerous felony either in the commission that makes it a dangerous felony or a felony dangerous by definition. It attaches liability for all foreseeable consequences of the felony. At common law, the felonies defined are burglary, arson, rape, robbery or kidnapping.

Here, the only possible felony involved would be robbery. As discussed previously, there was no force used to accomplish the taking and therefore cannot be a robbery.

REDLINE RULE EXCEPTION
Redline rule establishes that anyone on the right side of the line (police, victim, or bystander) that kills a felon or co-felon, the felon and co-felon would not be vicariously liable.

Here, Carla would be considered a victim or bystander because she was a security guard that worked for Friendly Market and was acting on their behalf. Carla would be considered someone on the right side of the line. Al was on the left side of the line because he was the felon in the commission of the crime. Because Carla was on the right side of the line and the death occurred of someone on the left side of the line, there is no vicarious liability.

Therefore, there is no malice aforethought.

Therefore, Beth cannot be found guilty of the murder of Al because there was no malice aforethought and if there were through the felony murder rule, it would be ruled out with the redline rule exception.

IS CARLA GUILTY OF MURDER?

MURDER OF AL?
Murder defined supra.

HOMICIDE
Homicide defined supra.

See previous discussion. Here, but for Carla shooting her gun Al would not be dead.

Therefore, there is a homicide.

MALICE AFORETHOUGHT
Malice aforethought defined supra. It is clear from the facts that Carla did not have any intent to cause serious bodily injury, nor did the killing occur during her commission of an inherently dangerous felony.

INTENT TO KILL
Intent to kill is having the knowledge or desire with substantial certainty that the result will occur.

Here, Carla had intent because she knew by shooting her weapon with careful aim there was a substantial certainty that it would result in Al's death.

DEADLY WEAPON DOCTRINE
Deadly weapon doctrine allows the inference of intent to kill when the weapon is an inherently dangerous weapon or it is used in the manner that makes it deadly.

Here, Carla fired a weapon with a warning shot. This wouldn't provide the inference of intent to kill. However, Carla didn't just fire a warning shot, she took the time to fire three shots. Here, Carla used the weapon in a deadly manner because she took careful aim to shoot Al. The second time she missed, but the third time she took careful aim and killed him. The weapon was used in an inherently dangerous manner because it resulted in Al's death.

Therefore, an inference of intent to kill can be made because Carla took careful aim while using a weapon.

WANTON CONDUCT
Wanton conduct defined supra.

Here, Carla had a disregard for human life because Al was running away from the store. He had halted the commission of his crime by exiting the store and running through the alley. Carla not only fired a warning shot which would get most reasonable people to stop but she continued firing. In her attempts on Al both times, she took careful aim of where she was shooting Al.

Therefore, Carla had wanton conduct.

Therefore, there is malice aforethought.

JUSTIFICATION, EXCUSE OR MITIGATIONS
If Carla can show that she has a justification or mitigation, she may not be liable for the death of Al. A justification, if proven successful, will turn the label of murder into no crime. A justification is established with crime prevention, apprehension of a fleeing felon, self-defense or defense of others, or a good faith reasonable mistake. An excuse can be found with infancy, insanity or intoxication. Carla wouldn't appear to have any excuses. A mitigation occurs through a provocation or criminal negligence.

CRIME PREVENTION
Crime prevention is allowed when you see the victim engaged in the commission of an inherently dangerous felony and the felon was fleeing the scene.

Here, Carla will argue that she was preventing the commission of a crime because Al was engaged in taking the beer that he didn't pay for from the store. Here, Carla will argue that Al was fleeing from the scene because Al was running from the store. However, Al didn't commit robbery because there was no force used to accomplish the taking, and he put the beer down before leaving the store.

Therefore, Carla would not be justified in crime prevention.

APPREHENSION OF A FLEEING FELON
You had a third element from crime prevention; the felon must pose a risk to police or the public.

Here, Al didn't pose any risk because Al wasn't armed. Therefore, Carla wouldn't be justified in apprehension of a fleeing felon.

Therefore, Carla would not have any justifications, excuses, or mitigations.

FIRST-DEGREE MURDER
At common law, there were no degrees of murder. Modernly, degrees have been established to provide harsher punishments for harsher crimes. First-degree murder can be found with premeditation and deliberation or a killing during the commission of an inherently dangerous felony. It is clear that Carla was not engaged in the commission of an inherently dangerous felony.

PREMEDITATION & DELIBERATION

Premeditation occurs with a thought and plan and continues with the plan. Deliberation occurs with a cool mind and time to reflect about the consequences.

Here, there was premeditation because Carla took careful aim when shooting at Al. Carla shot more than one time while Al was running for his safety. Here, there was deliberation because after Carla missed on the second shot, she paused, took careful aim and shot again. At the moment that Carla paused, she had a cool mind while she was setting up her third shot (second attempt at Al). She shot with deliberate purpose to kill him, not to injure him.

Therefore, Carla would be found guilty of murder because she did not have any justifications, excuses or mitigations. If this was a jurisdiction that followed first-degree murder, then Carla would be guilty of first-degree murder.

QUESTION 2

Dealer operates an antique shop. While traveling, she buys a Union cavalry officer's handgun for $1,500 from Seller. Dealer takes several photos of the handgun and Seller agrees to ship it to Dealer's shop. When Dealer arrives home, she immediately shows the photos of the handgun to Buyer. The parties shake hands on a deal to sell the handgun to Buyer for $2,000, payment upon delivery.

The next day, Buyer regrets agreeing to the deal without first having an opportunity to actually examine the handgun. Buyer tells Dealer that he will not pay the $2,000 unless she first allows him to have the handgun examined by an expert appraiser. Dealer becomes angry and tells Buyer, "A deal's a deal. I'll expect my money when the handgun is delivered to you."

When the handgun arrives at Dealer's shop, she does some internet research and discovers that the handgun was issued to a general who played a prominent role at the Battle of Gettysburg, which increases the value of the handgun by a factor of ten. The next day, Dealer receives a letter from Buyer stating, "Sorry. You're right. A deal's a deal." The envelope contains a check for $2,000. Dealer sends the check back to Buyer with a note stating, "Buyer: Because you backed out of our deal, I will not sell you the handgun. //Signed// Dealer."

A few weeks later, Buyer learns that Dealer is offering the handgun for sale at her shop for $20,000 because of its connection to the Civil War general. Buyer brings suit against Dealer for breach of contract, requesting specific performance.

1. Is Buyer likely to prevail against Dealer in his suit for breach of contract? Discuss.

2. If so, is the court likely to grant Buyer's request for specific performance? Discuss

QUESTION 2: SELECTED ANSWER A

Governing Law

The Uniform Commercial Code ("U.C.C.") governs contracts for the sale of goods -- tangible personal property not affixed to real property -- while the common law governs all other contracts, including those for personal services.

Here, the facts indicate that the deal in question is a handgun in exchange for money. A handgun is tangible and there is no indication that the handgun in question was permanently affixed to real estate.

The U.C.C. will govern this contract because it is for the sale of goods.

Merchant Rules

While the U.C.C. applies to all contracts for the sale of goods, some of the more stringent provisions apply only to deals where one or both of the parties are merchants.

Regarding Dealer, the facts indicate that Dealer "operates an antique shop." Since the item in question is an antique, it seems reasonable to conclude that Dealer is a merchant. The only factor that may lie against considering Dealer a merchant is that Dealer needed to research the item before obtaining its true value. Perhaps, Dealer could argue that this is evidence that he does not possess the requisite expertise to be qualified as a merchant.

However, balancing both sides, Dealer will likely be found to be a merchant.

Regarding Buyer, the facts do not indicate that Buyer is a merchant. We know nothing of Buyer other than that he agreed to purchase the gun.

Dealer will be held to merchant rules while Buyer will be held to non-merchant rules.

Buyer v. Dealer

Was There a Contract?

A contract is a set of promises that the law is prepared to enforce. There must be an offer, an acceptance, and mutual consideration.

Offer

An offer is an outward manifestation of present intent to be bound to a contract. Under the common law, an offer must sufficiently describe the parties, the subject matter, the quantity, the price, and the time of delivery. Under the U.C.C., however, price and time may be omitted and a court will substitute reasonable terms for those that are missing.

Here, Dealer showed Buyer pictures of the handgun and the facts state that they came to an agreement on a price of $2,000. The facts do not clearly identify whether the $2,000 offer was made by Dealer or Buyer.

An offer was made by either Dealer or Buyer.

Acceptance

An acceptance is an unequivocal agreement to be bound by the terms of an offer. Acceptance must be made while the offer is still outstanding and in the manner specified by the offeror, but if no manner specified, by a reasonable manner.

Here, the facts state that the parties "shook hands on a deal." Traditionally, this is a manifestation of agreement to terms. Since both parties shook hands, both parties agreed to the terms. It therefore matters not whether the offer was by Dealer for Buyer's acceptance, or by Buyer for Dealer's acceptance -- either way, it was accepted.

Since the parties immediately prior to the acceptance had verbally negotiated an offer, it would not appear that the offer was terminated before acceptance. Since the offer did not include a specified means of acceptance, the method of acceptance must be reasonable, and there are no facts that would indicate that a handshake was unreasonable. Indeed, since both offeror and offeree participated in the handshake, and offeror made no objection, it would seem that the offeror consented to that method of acceptance.

The offer was accepted by the offeree.

Consideration

Consideration is bargained-for legal detriment; "an agreement to do what one needn't, or to refrain from doing what one may."

Here, the facts show that Dealer was going to transfer ownership of the handgun to Buyer, which she had no obligation to do but for the contract. Likewise, Buyer was to transfer money to Dealer, which he had no obligation to do but for the contract. These obligations arose out of a negotiating, or bargaining, process, and constitute legal detriment.

There was mutual consideration. The contract was formed absent a defense.

Defense - Statute of Frauds

The Statute of Frauds requires a contract to be in writing if it is: 1) for the sale of goods valued at more than $500, 2) for the sale of an interest in land, 3) an agreement to answer for the debt of another, 4) impossible to complete within 1 year, *or* 5) in consideration of marriage.

Relevant to this contract is the first of these: the contract was for the sale of a handgun valued at (under the contract) $2,000. As such, the contract must be in writing to be enforceable, absent an exception.

U.C.C. Merchant's Confirmatory Memorandum

A contract that would otherwise be unenforceable under the Statute of Frauds may still be enforceable if a merchant seller issues a signed writing confirming the deal.

As discussed *supra*, Dealer is a merchant, and in this transaction, she is the seller. The facts state that Dealer sent Buyer a note that referred to the deal. The note was signed. Dealer will argue that this is insufficient to constitute a confirmatory memorandum because he specifically wrote that the deal is off. However, any signed writing by a merchant seller that evidences the existence of a contract is sufficient to apply this exception to the Statute of Frauds.

The merchant's confirmatory memorandum exception applies, and Dealer will not be able to escape liability under the Statute of Frauds.

Defense - Anticipatory Repudiation

An anticipatory repudiation is a definite, unequivocal manifestation by a party to a contract that they will not perform one or more of their duties under that contract. The non-repudiating party may treat the repudiation as an immediate material breach of contract or may demand that the repudiating party perform as agreed. And, if the repudiating party is in breach, the non-repudiating party's duties are discharged, thus providing Dealer a defense if he can prove that Buyer breached first.

This defense presents two issues for Dealer. First, a request to have the item inspected before purchase may not be sufficiently definite and unequivocal of a manifestation that one intends to fail to perform their duties. Dealer will argue that Buyer's statement that he "will not pay ... unless" Dealer did something he was under no obligation to do is sufficiently clear as to Dealer's intent to breach. Buyer will argue that his statement is mere grumbling and does not rise to the definiteness required to be an anticipatory repudiation. Dealer probably has the better of these arguments. However, it seems Dealer elected to demand assurances rather than treat this as an immediate breach by telling Buyer that he "expect[s]" the Buyer to go through with the deal. Buyer then provided assurance that he would perform, *before* he gave any notice of intent to treat the anticipatory repudiation as a breach.

To the extent that Buyer repudiated the contract, he cured that repudiation with his letter assuring performance, and Dealer will not be able to escape liability under a theory of anticipatory repudiation.

Defense - Mistake

A mutual mistake is when, at the formation of the contract, the parties are mistaken as to a fact that goes to the essence of the bargain, and the risk of such a mistake was not placed on the parties under the express or implied terms. Such a contract is voidable by either party.

Here, it seems that neither party knew the value of the handgun at contract formation. Dealer was originally going to sell it for one tenth of what it should have been, while Buyer almost backed out of the deal. The mistake in the value of the handgun is therefore mutual. Dealer will argue that this mistake was as to the essence of the bargain; that is, the contract was for an ordinary Civil War handgun, not for a general's weapon. Buyer will argue that the risk of an antique being more or less valuable as a result of learning more about the history of that antique is inherent in the transaction and not a risk that the parties should not bear. Or, being that Dealer is a merchant,

Buyer may argue that the risk he created for himself by failing to exercise caution by researching before selling, as he should have known to do as a merchant of antiques, is Dealer's fault and Dealer's to bear. Further, Buyer could argue that Dealer's mistake was not reasonable, as Dealer could have learned of the issue by doing some basic Internet searching as he later did.

Due to the nature of antiques and the Dealer's failure to research before selling, it is unlikely Dealer will be able to escape liability under a theory of mutual mistake.

Specific Performance

Specific performance is an equitable remedy reserved for when money damages are insufficient to make a plaintiff whole. Equitable remedies are never given as-of-right -- they are at the discretion of the court.

Here, the facts indicate that the handgun is, essentially, one-of-a-kind. No amount of money can purchase a replacement of it, as the item's value is not in the metal the handgun contains, nor in the cost to turn metal into a handgun, but in the historical nature of the item, and history cannot be bought.

The court should grant Buyer's request for specific performance.

Other Remedy

If the court refuses to exercise its discretion to issue equitable relief, Buyer may seek expectation damages. Expectation damages seek to give the non-breaching party the "benefit of the bargain;" that is, to put them in the position that they would have been had the contract been fulfilled.

The benefit of the bargain can be calculated as the market value of what the plaintiff would have received minus the expenses the plaintiff would have had if the contract had gone through. The facts suggest that the market value may be $20,000 due to the listing price by the dealer and the 10x enhancement of value from the $2,000 original price. A court would make the final determination as to the fair market value.

Assuming that value is $20,000, Buyer's expenses would have been $2,000, and Buyer would be entitled to $18,000 in expectation damages if the court declines to issue equitable relief.

QUESTION 2: SELECTED ANSWER B

I. Will Buyer likely prevail against Dealer for breach? What is the applicable law?

The law that applies for a contract involving the sale of goods is the UCC. The UCC will apply here because the contract concerns the sale of a good, the gun.

A. Was contract formed?

A contract is a promise or set of promises for which the law will provide a remedy for its breach. A contract is formed when there is mutual assent, consideration, and no defenses to its enforcement.

1. **Mutual assent** is where there is a valid offer that is accepted.

a. **Offer** is a commitment of intent to be bound by the promisor that contains the material terms of the offer, that is communicated to an identified offeree, that invites acceptance. The UCC states that the quantity is the only material term needed for an offer. Here we have Dealer showing pictures of a Union cavalry officer's handgun to Buyer directly, and offering to sell it to him for $2000. This is a valid offer

b. **Acceptance**: a commitment from the promisee to be bound to the terms of the offer that is communicated back by either promise or performance of promise. Here, the buyer promises to purchase the gun, and they shake hands in apparent agreement. This offer was accepted. Valid mutual assent exists between the parties.

2. **Consideration** – a bargained-for exchange between the parties that produces a legal detriment. The bargained-for exchange is where the parties are each bargaining for something that they would like. Dealer is bargaining to give the gun to Buyer in exchange for a payment of $2000. The legal detriment occurs when the party either promises to do something that they are not already legally obligated to do, or when they refrain from doing something that they are legally entitled to do. Dealer giving the gun to Buyer and Buyer paying the $2000 is good legal detriment. This is good consideration.

3. **Defenses to enforcement**: if the party can show a defense that is valid the Court will not enforce the contract.

a. **Statute of Frauds** – the statute of frauds requires tangible evidence that a contract exists to make it enforceable for some of the more easily imagined types of contracts. One of these types is a contract for the sale of goods for $500 or more. The tangible evidence needed is a writing signed by the party to be charged, a partial performance on the contract, or a reasonable foreseeable detrimental reliance (promissory estoppel) on the contract.

The writing must evidence the material terms of the contract and be signed by the party to be charged. Our tangible evidence in this case, would be the letter that was signed by the Dealer that states "Buyer: Because you backed out of our deal, I will not sell you the handgun." This writing states that they did have a deal. This would suffice to remove this contract from the statute of frauds and this would not succeed as a defense.

B. What effect does Buyer telling the Dealer he will not pay without first having the gun examined have?

1. *Anticipatory Repudiation* – when one party unequivocally states that they will not perform their duties under a contract before performance is due that is an anticipatory breach. The issue here is whether Buyer was absolutely refusing to perform. He is just stating that he wants the gun examined by an appraiser first. He is not in definite terms stating he will not pay the money. This is not definite enough language to be construed as an unequivocal refusal to perform.

2. *Modification* – a modification is when a party seeks to change the terms of an existing contract. Here, the buyer wants to add in a condition that the gun is examined before he will pay. The UCC treats a modification with new terms as a separate term that can either be accepted or rejected by the other party. When the Dealer becomes angry and says "A deal is a deal. I'll expect my money when the handgun is delivered to you," she is refusing outright to accept these terms.

Had the modification been accepted, if it was deemed to be out of good faith it would not require new consideration, but it was not accepted so terms stay as is.

C. *Performance of the contract*: When any conditions are met or excused, the duties of the parties come due. If these duties are not performed then the result is a breach of contract, <u>unless</u> the duties can be discharged.

1. *Discharge of duties when the party due to perform claims that they cannot because of an unforeseen event* that has occurred. Impossibility is when the party states that it is impossible for them to perform. This impossibility must be objective, to where no one in the world could perform the duty. There are no facts to support this. Impracticability is when the party claims that performance would give them a substantial hardship.

Here, Dealer does not want to perform because she now knows how much the gun is actually worth, so selling it for the contract price would limit her profit by 10x what she could get. While this loss is substantial, the party in a sale assumes the risk of a profit loss due to making a bad deal. This argument would not work to discharge her duties. It is likely that when Dealer refused to sell the gun and Buyer tendered his payment of the $2000 that she was in breach. – – –

3. **Mistake**. The last chance Dealer would have to avoid the contract would be that she was mistaken as to the true value of the gun. A unilateral mistake where only one party is mistaken will have no effect unless the other party knew or should have known of the mistake. Here, Dealer was the one selling the gun and Buyer was just someone she showed pictures to. His reluctance to purchase without an appraisal shows he did not know and probably didn't have reason to. Mutual mistake where both parties are mistaken as to a material term of contract can make the contract voidable by either party. If Dealer could assert that they both were mistaken as to the value of the gun, – this could have the effect of making it voidable. She should try to argue this, as this is her only hope. She will

be deemed, as an antique dealer, to have assumed this risk and it won't be successful.

II. Can Buyer get specific performance?

A. **Specific performance** is a remedy in which the party is seeking the contract to be ordered to be performed. Specific performance is only applicable when monetary damages wouldn't be adequate or if the subject matter is truly unique.

If the Buyer could argue that this Union cavalry officer's gun was unique because it was issued to a general who played a prominent role at the Battle of Gettysburg, then the court could decide to order Dealer to sell it to him. Courts will avoid this where it would cause them too much supervising. Being that the gun is so unique, he may have a chance at a decree of specific performance.

QUESTION 3

Barry is a licensed barber. Recently, he has considered changing from the straight razor that he has always used to a new type of electric razor. The primary advantage of the new razor is that it totally eliminates the possibility of the customer being cut in the process of getting a shave.

In general, barbers prefer the tradition of using the straight razor to the electric razor because it allows them to better show off their skills as a barber. Although not all agree, some believe that the straight razor gives a closer shave.

The new razors have, however, been scientifically established to provide just as close a shave as the straight razor.

Barry continues to shave men as he always has because he enjoys the use of the blade, and because the electric razor is expensive. He is also concerned about the reliability of these new devices under the heavy use they would receive in a barbershop.

Moe comes into Barry's shop to get a shave. Halfway through the shave, Moe suddenly jumps up from the chair, cheering because he checked his smartphone and saw his favorite baseball team score a run. In the process,

Barry's razor creates a fairly deep gash on Moe's throat.

Moe punches Barry, giving him a black eye.

1. Is Moe likely to prevail on a negligence claim against Barry? Discuss.

2. Is Barry likely to prevail on an intentional tort claim against Moe? Discuss.

QUESTION 3: SELECTED ANSWER A

MOE V. BARRY

Negligence - To prevail in a claim for negligence a plaintiff must prove duty, breach of the duty, actual and proximate (legal) causation, and damages.

Duty - Defendants owe a duty of due care to all foreseeable plaintiffs. Here, Barry is a licensed barber who provides shaves to men. Barry has a duty to protect his patrons (foreseeable plaintiffs) against harm for the services he provides.

Standard of Care - Here, Barry is a licensed barber; here, the standard of care is that of a licensed barber in the same or similar circumstances. The facts indicate, however, that in general barbers prefer the tradition of using the straight razor because many agree it provides a closer shave and allows them to show off their barbering skills. Barry could argue that his use of a straight razor is common in the industry and is customary.

Breach - Breach of duty is demonstrated when the care used by defendant falls below the standard. Breach of duty can be found when weighing the probability and magnitude of the harm vs. the burden and utility.

Here, Barry has considered hanging from the straight razor he always used to an electric razor. He opted not to change because he enjoys using the blade and the electric razor is expensive and he has concerns about the reliability of the devices. The new electric razor totally eliminates the possibility of a customer being cut while receiving a shave and science has proven that the shave is just as close as with a straight razor. The probability of the harm and magnitude of harm from using a straight razor when weighed against the burden on Barry of purchasing and using an electric razor is great. The likelihood he will cut people while shaving with a blade is greater and the harm greater than using an electric razor.

The social utility of an electric razor is significant in that cuts are less likely to occur. When weighing the probability and magnitude of harm against the burden on Barry to purchase and use an electric razor, combined with the utility of the razor in that it completely eliminates risk of cuts and provides just as good a shave as a straight razor, Barry has breached his duty.

Causation - Actual - Actual Cause is established by use of the "but-for" test. But for Barry's action of using a straight razor, Moe's injuries would not have occurred. If Barry had used an electric razor, the possibility of Moe being cut was eliminated. Barry is the actual cause of Moe's injuries.

Causation - Proximate - Proximate (or Legal) Cause is an analysis of the foreseeability of the type and extent of plaintiff's harm. Here, Moe is a foreseeable plaintiff and the type of injury he sustained is foreseeable. Moe was receiving a shave from Barry with a straight razor; it is foreseeable that in the process of shaving that someone might be cut, even more than a minor cut based upon the dangerousness of the straight edge razor. Further, there were not intervening or superseding events to break the causal chain. Barry is the proximate (legal) cause of Moe's injuries.

Damages - For a claim in negligence, plaintiff must have suffered damages. Here, Moe suffered damage; he received a fairly deep gash on his throat due to a cut from Barry's straight razor.

Defenses

Contributory Negligence - In jurisdictions that allow contributory negligence defenses, any fault on plaintiff's part that contributed to his/her own injuries would act as a complete bar to recovery. Here, the facts indicate Moe jumped up suddenly from the chair when checking his smartphone because his favorite baseball team scored a run. A court may find that Moe's actions were a significant factor in contributing to the injury he suffered; if so, Moe's claim would be barred and Barry would have no liability.

Comparative Negligence - In a jurisdiction that recognizes comparative fault, fault would be apportioned to both Moe and Barry in relation to their proportionate share of contributing to the injury. In a pure comparative fault situation, the parties would each be attributed a percentage of fault and Moe's recovery from Barry would be reduced by that amount (for example, Moe was 80% at fault and Barry was 20% at fault and Moe's damages were determined to be $10,000, Moe's recovery would be reduced by $2,000). In a modified comparative fault, if Moe was found to be more than 50% responsible for his own injuries, he would not recover damages. If Moe's actions of jumping up suddenly from the chair in response to his team's scoring a run, he will likely be found to have some liability for his own injury and will be allocated a share of fault. That share of fault will determine whether he will recover based upon pure comparative or modified comparative fault.

Assumption of the Risk - Assumption of the risk is a valid defense when the plaintiff knowingly and voluntarily either expressly or impliedly consented to the activity that caused harm.

Here, it could be argued that Moe assumed the risk he would be cut by Barry during a shave with a straight razor. Moe's consent to the shave is implied because he voluntarily entered Barry's shop for a shave and consented to the activity.

Moe is likely to prevail on a claim of negligence against Barry because he had a duty, that duty was breached because the probability and magnitude of harm was greater than the burden and utility of using an electric razor rather than a straight razor, Barry was both the actual and proximate cause of Moe's harm, and Moe suffered injury. Moe is likely to prevail on a negligence claim against Barry. Moe's damages are likely to be minimized if fault is apportioned between Moe and Barry in response to Moe's actions in jumping up from the chair.

BARRY V. MOE

Battery - an intentional volitional act resulting in a harmful or offensive touching.

Intentional - Intent is the desire or knowledge with substantial certainty that the act will bring about the desired outcome. Here, the facts indicate that Moe punched Barry; Moe's act of punching Barry was intentional. This element of battery is met.

Volitional Act - Voluntary, not reflexive action - Here, the facts indicate that Moe punched Barry. Moe may argue that it was not a volitional act but rather was reflexive in nature due to being cut on his throat by Barry. Because Barry suffered a black eye, it would appear that there was some aim on Moe's part; accordingly, his claim that it was not a volitional act would likely fail. The volitional element of battery is met.

Harmful or Offensive Touching - Here, the facts indicate that Moe punched Barry giving him a black eye. The touching was both harmful (black eye) and offensive (humiliating). The element of battery is met.

Defense - Self-Defense - Moe may attempt to claim he was defending himself against Barry when he punched him in the face. In the excitement of the moment, Moe may not have realized that if he jumped up while Barry was shaving him that he was likely to be injured. Further, in the same excitement, he may not have realized what occurred and was reacting to being cut. This defense is likely to fail.

Moe is likely to prevail on an intentional tort claim of battery against Moe.

QUESTION 3: SELECTED ANSWER B

1. Negligence of Barry:

For Moe to succeed in a claim against Barry for negligence, he would need to prove the following elements:

    a. Duty: One who engages in an affirmative act owes a duty of due care to all foreseeable victims in the zone of danger created by the affirmative acts. In the current case, Barry is a licensed barber and has presumably gone through a rigorous and appropriate training program and had to pass certain tests, in addition to having to take affirmative steps to maintain his license as current and in good standing. As such, he may have a heightened duty to his customers above the general duty of due care given his special expertise. As such, Barry owes a duty of a reasonable licensed barber in the same or similar circumstances.

    b. Breach: It is a breach of duty if the defendant's conduct fell below the standard of care set forth by his or her duty

        1. Use of razor: In the facts, it is stated that barbers prefer the use of the straight razor and that Barry himself has always used it. There is scientific evidence that the straight razor provides as close a shave as the electric razor. There is evidence that the electric razor is more expensive and requires greater care and maintenance. It is also stated that the electric razor completely eliminates the risk of laceration. To determine whether the use of the razor falls below the standard of

care, one must utilize the Hand Formula to analyze. Here, a breach is found where the burden of using the electric razor is less than the risk of injury created by the standard blade, factoring in the utility of each. Here, the typical risk of injury is probably a minor cut rather than a deep laceration, however, given a sharp blade, as in the instant case, deep laceration is a risk. If the risk and likelihood of injury are significant and the burden to change to a safer approach is less significant, using the razor blade may be a breach of the standard of care. As it is stated that the performance of both are equal and there is some risk associated with the blade and no risk with the electric, the issue of standard of care would turn on the burden of buying and maintaining the electric versus the utility of each. If it can be shown that the burden is significant, there is not breach. Here, the electric is expensive and requires maintenance, but once you have one and can utilize it properly, it seems likely that the burden would not outweigh the potential risk of serious injury, given that a sharp razor blade is used about the face and may result in disfiguring injury or something serious like severing an artery. It can also be concluded, however, that if the risk of injury with razor blades is so significant, the industry standard would move away from this. Given the facts shown, it appears that continuing use of the razor blade would not sufficiently fall below the standard of care to amount to negligence.

    2. Laceration: The next question is whether Barry cutting Moe was negligent. If it is shown that Barry did not exercise that reasonable amount of care to prevent Moe from being cut, then his conduct fell below the standard of care. Here, the cut occurred with a sudden movement of Moe. If it is shown that Barry was

unreasonable in not keeping Moe still or in not warning him that he should not move suddenly while being shaved, or that he should have requested that Moe not use his smartphone while being shaved, Moe may have an argument for breach of duty.

c. Causation: To be found liable for negligence, it must be shown that Barry was the actual and legal cause of Moe's injuries. But for Barry's use of the razor when shaving Moe, Moe would not have been cut. However, the sudden movement of Moe while being shaved may be an intervening event that cuts off causation if it was unforeseeable. It seems that it would be foreseeable that someone might move while being shaved. Here, Moe was watching a baseball game on his smartphone. Barry should have foreseen the possibility that Moe might move suddenly in response to an event during the game to which Moe reacted. Because this was foreseeable, Moe's sudden movement would not be an intervening event which would cut off causation.

d. Harm: Here, Moe suffered a laceration on this throat.

e. Defenses: Barry could assert several defenses:

1. Contributory/Comparative Fault: If the jurisdiction follows the minority view of contributory negligence, any negligence on the part of Moe would cut off his ability to recover from Barry. If it was determined that Moe's sudden movement while being shaved with a razor blade was negligent, he would not be able to recover. If the jurisdiction follows the majority view of comparative fault, any negligence on the part of Moe

could reduce his recovery proportional to the level of his fault.

  2. Assumption of the risk: Assumption of the risk requires 2 elements. Moe must have known and realized the risks of getting shaved with a razor blade and knowing this risk, voluntarily participated in the activity. If Barry can show that Moe knew of the risks of getting cut while shaving and he continued to get shaved with the razor knowing these risks, he may succeed in his defense of AOR.

 f. Conclusion: Barry owed Moe a duty and breached that duty when he cut Moe with the razor which was the actual and proximate cause of Moe's injuries. However, Barry would likely succeed in his assertion of either defense of contributory negligence to reduce his liability (or comparative fault to eliminate it) or assumption of the risk by Moe. Moe's negligence action against Barry would not succeed.

2. Intentional Tort action against Moe

 a. Battery: Battery is a volitional act done with the intent to cause a harmful or offensive touching or with substantial certainly that a harmful or offensive touching will result.

  1. Volitional act: Moe punched Barry; there are no facts to suggest this was reflexive or otherwise not volitional.

2. Intentional: The intent element is satisfied where Moe intended the consequences of his actions or was substantially certain the consequences would result. Here Moe punched Barry after Barry cut Moe with the razor. It would appear this was done in retaliation for being cut. No facts are presented to suggest it was not Moe's intention to hit Barry.

3. Harmful or offensive touching: As judged by an objective standard, most everyone would consider being punched in the face as harmful or offensive. The fact that Barry received a black eye is proof of injury.

b. Assault: Assault is a volitional act done with the intent to cause reasonable apprehension of an imminent battery.

1. Volitional act: see above

2. Intent: Here, the intent element is met the same way; however, intent can transfer. If Moe's intent was to cause a battery and also caused reasonable apprehension of that battery, he has met the intent element for assault as well.

3. Reasonable apprehension: If Barry was aware that Moe was in the process of hitting him and this caused in him an apprehension that he is about to be struck, this would meet the element for the tort. It is judged on an objective standard and most people would likely find someone trying to hit them as causing apprehension.

b. No other intentional torts appear to have been committed by Moe.

c. Conclusion: Moe would be found liable for assault and battery of Barry.

QUESTION 4

Owner wants to turn her warehouse into a restaurant. She decides to install an innovative solar heating system, which Contractor agrees to install at a cost of $50,000. Contractor's son ("Son") wants to use two parking spaces in the warehouse parking lot for his (Son's) business. If Owner agrees to designate two parking spaces for Son's use for five years, Contractor will drop the price to $35,000.

On November 13th, the parties agree to the latter arrangement in a valid written contract in which Contractor promises to start the job on November 17th and to complete it by January 1st. The contract includes a recital stating, "Timely performance by Contractor is important to avoid any delay in the opening of Owner's restaurant."

State law requires that all installations of the new solar systems be done by a certified solar technician. On November 15th, the only certified technician who works for Contractor, Tech, is injured in a car accident. Contractor immediately notifies Owner and advises her that the start of the work will be delayed because of Tech's accident.

Owner replies, "You know that on-time performance is crucial. Yesterday, the city announced special tax breaks for businesses that open by the end of the year. Can you still finish by then?" Contractor says, "I don't know when we can start. It depends on how quickly Tech recovers."

Owner tells Contractor that she is terminating the contract.

Owner finds an alternative supplier of a similar system at a cost of $60,000, but he can't start work immediately and the restaurant opens in February of the following year.

Owner misses the deadline for the city tax break.

Owner sues Contractor for breach of contract.

Son sues Owner for breach of contract, seeking damages for Owner's failure to provide the two parking spaces.

1. Can Owner prevail in her lawsuit against Contractor? Discuss.

2. If so, can Owner recover a. The $10,000 in increased costs for the heating system? Discuss. b. The lost profits for the delay in opening the restaurant? Discuss. c. The value of the tax reduction? Discuss.

3. Can Son prevail in his lawsuit against Owner? Discuss.

QUESTION 4: SELECTED ANSWER A

Can Owner prevail in his lawsuit against Contractor?

UCC/Common law
UCC governs contract for the sale of goods. Common law governs all other contracts.

Goods: Tangible, movable items, identifiable at the time of sale

The contract is for the installation of the heating system. It could be argued that the contract price includes the price of the unit itself, and that it is therefore a contract for the sale of goods. However, the facts state that the contract was for the installation of the unit, which indicated that the purchase of the unit is merely incidental to the terms. The court will evaluate this based on a test of what the major value of the contract is from. In this case, particularly since the law requires a specialist to install the unit, it seems clear that the installation of the unit is likely the major value of the contract price.

Thus, the common law will govern.

Formation

Offer
An outward manifestation of present contractual intent, clear and definite in terms and communicated to the offeree in such a way as to create a reasonable expectation that the offeror is willing to enter into a contract.

Offer 1:
The facts indicate that the original offer was for $50,000 and contained no parking spaces. While this was a valid offer as it contained the other terms as outlined below, the facts indicate also that there was a modification of the contract.

Modification of contract
The facts state that there was an offer based on the original terms which were agreed to. However, the facts also state that the parties later agreed to reduce the price to $35,000 in exchange for O adding two parking spaces to the deal. Because the change in price and the addition of the spaces was new consideration, this modification will be valid. The facts state that it was valid.

In this case, the terms of the offer are:

Quantity: 1 installation and 2 parking spaces
Time for Performance: Nov 17-Jan 1
Identity of the parties: O and C
Price: $35,000
Subject matter: Installation of a heating unit

Acceptance
<u>An outward manifestation of unequivocal assent to the terms of the offer</u>.

There are no issues to discuss here. The facts state that there was a valid offer and acceptance.

Consideration
The bargained-for exchange of legal benefit and legal detriment between parties.

There are no issues to discuss here. The facts state that the contract was valid, which required consideration. The consideration would be the installation of the unit and the receipt of two parking spaces in exchange for $35,000.

There is valid consideration.

Defenses
The facts state that it was a valid written contract. There are no defenses to the enforcement of the contract.

Conditions
An act or event not certain to occur which, if it does occur, gives rise to or extinguishes a legal duty.

Express
O will argue that there was an express condition precedent to O's duty to pay that the installation be started by Nov. 12 and completed by Jan. 1. The court will typically construe a given term to be a promise rather than a condition unless it is clear from the terms that the intent of the parties was for a duty to not arise unless the condition was met. In the event of a time for performance, the courts typically will not find an express condition unless there is a "time of the essence" clause included.

Here, O will argue that the contract clearly states that the performance must begin and finish on time because they are trying to avoid delay in opening. This could be considered sufficient, but it does not clearly state that the duty of O is conditioned on such event; rather it outlines the importance and makes clear that C is required to perform.

The court could find this to be an express condition precedent, but more likely it will be construed as a promise by C.

Implied in fact
There are no implied-in-fact conditions.

Implied in law
The law assumes a condition precedent that the longer performance will be done before the shorter performance. Thus, in this case the duty of O to pay will be conditioned on the installation of the unit by C.

This condition was never met by C.

Duties
C had the duty to install the unit.

O had the duty to pay $35,000 and to allow the use of 2 parking spaces.

Excuse of duties: Impossibility/impracticability
C will argue that his duty to perform was legitimately delayed by his only certified worker becoming sick. If this argument prevails then C will be allowed to delay performance until impossibility is removed. The law requires the certified worker to be the one to install the unit. In this case, it is possible that C could have subcontracted with another worker, but the facts are not

clear as to whether or not it was feasible to do or if this would have delayed completion of the installation.

It is possible that C will prevail on this argument, since the law prevented him from using his technicians, but O will argue that C assumed this risk by hiring only one technician when he knew that a certified technician was required. The court would likely agree with this argument because C should have foreseen this risk prior to contracting, and thus implicitly assumed it.

This excuse will likely fail.

Frustration of purpose
O could argue that the purpose of the contract was frustrated because he was not able to complete in time to gain the necessary tax breaks. However, this argument will almost certainly fail because the facts do not indicate that this purpose was discussed between O and C prior to contracting. The court will require the purpose of the contract to have been completed by both parties before it will allow this excuse to prevail.

This excuse will fail.

Breach
The facts state that C told O that he was unable to perform in time because his technician was injured. Unless C's duty to perform on time was excused/delayed above, then this will be at least an anticipatory repudiation of the agreement, and possibly a major breach.

Anticipatory breach
O will argue that the statement by C that he "did not know" when he could begin was a major breach, or at least that

his first statement that they would not begin on time was. However, because there were still two days left to begin performance and because it was still possible for C to perform in time, this would likely not be a complete repudiation. Thus, it would give rise to the right by O to demand assurances of performance. The facts state that O did just that when he asked "Can you still finish by then?"

C was unable to provide these assurances, which would allow O to sue for breach, unless the duty to perform on time was excused above.

Conclusion
It is likely that C is in breach on contract because is it likely that his duty was not excused, since he assumed the risk. Thus, his inability to provide assurances constitutes an anticipatory breach by C and allows O to sue for damages.

Can Son prevail in his lawsuit against Owner?

Third-party rights
Beneficiaries
intended beneficiary

The facts indicate that Son was an intended beneficiary of the O and C contract. The contract stated that S would receive 2 parking spaces for 5 years. An intended beneficiary can sue based on a breach of contract if his rights have vested. In this case, the facts are not clear as to whether S's rights have vested because they do not indicate whether he has relied or confirmed his understanding and acceptance of the arrangement. However, it is reasonable to assume that S would have been aware of the arrangement and would have consented because his father was the contractor.

O will be allowed to raise any defenses against S that he would have been able to raise against C. In this case, if C is found to have anticipatorily breached the contract then O will be able to use this as a defense against S and refuse to perform on the contract to S as well.

It is likely that C will be found to have anticipatorily breached, and thus O will be able to refuse performance to S and S will not be able to recover against Owner.

Can Owner prevail for $10,000 for the heating system, the lost profit on the restaurant, or the value of the tax reduction?

Remedies
General Damages
Expectation

Expectation damages are designed to put the injured party back in the position they would have been in had the contract been performed. In this case, O was contracted to pay C $35,000, but this price included the use of 2 parking spaces by C. The original contract was going to cost O $50,000. O was scheduled to receive the installation of the unit. The court cannot fully compensate C through expectation damages because C was expecting an installation, and the court will not require specific performance on a personal service contract.

Cover.

The court will allow O to "cover" his damages by contracting with someone else to provide what C was not able to. Thus, O will be able to recover the difference between the cost of his new contract and the cost of his original contract. The court will likely estimate this against the $50,000 figure which was originally agreed to, because the $35,000 figure included the use of two parking spaces.

O will likely be able to recover the $10,000 extra that was spent under the new contract.

Duty to mitigate

O has the duty to mitigate his damages to prevent any unreasonable and foreseeable increase in damages which could have been avoided. The facts are not clear as to whether or not O tried to find cheaper contractors before agreeing to the price of $60,000. However, considering that O was trying hard to get the work done quickly presumably he contacted multiple contractors and picked the one that was the best balance of price and timeliness.

If O failed to mitigate then C would be able to reduce the damages by the amount which O could reasonably have avoided.

Consequential

Lost profits on the restaurant are most likely not recoverable. The court will usually only allow recovery for lost profits if it is an established business where the profits can be reasonably estimated, and if the damage was reasonably foreseeable by both parties. While the damage was reasonably foreseeable, because this restaurant was brand new, there is no good way to estimate the profits which were lost. Thus, O will not be able to recover for lost profits.

Reliance
O will argue that he relied on C's representations that work would be finished by Jan 1 and that he was damaged by the fact that work was not finished on time, causing him to lose the tax breaks. However, this argument will fail because, while O did fail to gain the tax breaks, this was not contemplated prior to the contract and, therefore, O did not rely on that representation.

Conclusion
O will be able to recover $10,000 for the cost of the new heating system, will not be able to recover the lost profits on the restaurant, and will not be able to recover for the loss of the tax breaks.

QUESTION 4: SELECTED ANSWER B

OWNER v. CONTRACTOR

GOVERNING LAW
All contracts for the sale of goods are governed by the UCC. Goods are movable and tangible items at the time of identification of a contract. All contracts not governed by the UCC are governed by the common law.

HYBRID CONTRACT
Here the subject matter of the contract is for the purchase and installation of a solar heating system. The majority of jurisdictions will determine whether the thrust of the contract was for goods or services and use the thrust as the basis for determining governing law. A minority of jurisdictions apply the Gravamen test where the goods portion of the contract is governed by the UCC and the services component is governed by the common law.

Here, it is likely that the thrust of the contract will be established to be services since the installation was solicited and quoted, specifically.

Therefore, this contract will be governed by the common law.

CONTRACT FORMATION
A valid contract consists of offer, acceptance, consideration and no defenses.

MUTUAL ASSENT
Where, the parties through a written agreement and/or their conduct, have expressly or impliedly demonstrated a

mutual intent to be bound to the terms of a contract, mutual assent (consisting of a valid offer and acceptance) can be demonstrated.

Here, the parties have a written contract for the installation of a solar system and it contains the necessary terms of parties, price ($35K plus 5 years use of parking space), quantity and subject matter (one solar system installation), and time of performance (beginning November 17 and completed by January 1).

Mutual assent can be demonstrated.

CONSIDERATION
Consideration is a legally sufficient bargained-for exchange between the parties requiring a valid benefit and/or detriment.

Here, Owner was to pay $35,000 and provide two parking spaces for 5 years in exchange for installation of a solar system.

This is legally sufficient consideration.

DEFENSES TO FORMATION
STATUTE OF FRAUDS
The statute of frauds is a set of rules that requires certain types of contracts to be in writing and signed by the party to be charged. The only relevant rule under SOF would be if this contract could not be performed in a year, which is not the case here.

Therefore, the statute of frauds will not be a defense to formation.

Therefore, barring any defenses, there is an enforceable contract between Owner and Contractor.

THIRD-PARTY BENEFICIARIES

A third-party beneficiary is one the parties to a contract intend to confer a benefit on at the time of contracting. To have standing to sue upon the contract, it must be shown that the parties intended him to benefit and his rights must have vested. A *donee beneficiary* is one that receives the benefit gratuitously and his rights do not vest until he materially changes his position in reliance upon the promise. A *creditor beneficiary* is one where there is a duty owed and its rights vest when it learns of the right, changes its position, or sues to seek enforcement of the promise. Incidental beneficiaries have no standing to sue on the contract.

Here, Son was a third-party beneficiary of the contract between Owner and Contractor because the contract specifically named him and indicated that they intended to confer the benefit of the use of two parking spaces to him.

Son is a third-party beneficiary of the contract between Owner and Contractor.

PERFORMANCE
CONDITIONS
TIME OF ESSENCE

Where a contract unequivocally states specific dates in which the contract must be performed, time is of the essence and failure to deliver duties in that period is considered a material breach.

Here, within the contract, it states that "Contractor promises to start the job on November 17 and complete it by January 1st." Owner will argue that it is unequivocal because it uses the words "promises to" which establishes an absolute duty to perform within that window.

Furthermore, Contractor agreed to the terms during contracting without objection.

This contract contains a time is of the essence clause.

BREACH
Breach is the failure to perform a duty under the contract. A minor breach is when the breaching party has substantially performed under the contract, but not perfectly. A major breach is when the non-performance of the duty substantially impairs the expected benefit of the bargain for the non-breaching party.

PROSPECTIVE INABILITY TO PERFORM
Where a party, through its words or conduct indicates that it may not be able to perform its duties under the contract or non-breaching party has reason to suspect he will not, non-breaching party can demand assurance. If adequate assurance is not received, non-breaching party can terminate its own performance and sue for damages.

Here, Contractor contacts Owner on Nov 15, two days before job is scheduled to start, stating that the only possible installer has been injured and cannot perform within the time specified in the contract. When Owner demanded assurance, Contractor failed to provide adequate assurance that it would perform.

Therefore, Contractor has unequivocally repudiated and breached its duties under the contract. Owner can sue immediately.

DEFENSES
IMPOSSIBILITY OF PERFORMANCE
Where the performance of duties due under a contract becomes objectively impossible, a breaching party may be excused from performance and all other duties terminated.

Here, Contractor will argue that it was impossible to perform within the time frame specified in the contract due to the injury of the technician. He will argue that because state law requires them to be certified, replacements are not easy to find and his performance was, therefore, impossible.

Owner will argue that injury to a technician, especially when you have only one, is foreseeable and that this was a risk assumed by Contractor. Owner will also argue that it is not objectively impossible to find an alternate installer, even if it costs substantially more.

A court would likely agree and find that performance by Contractor of its duties was not impossible and he will not be excused from performing his duties.

REMEDIES
EQUITABLE REMEDIES

SPECIFIC PERFORMANCE
Where the subject matter is unique and monetary damages are inadequate, a court may order a party to perform under a contract.

Because this is a contract for services, a court will not order specific performance since monetary damages will be adequate.

COMPENSATORY DAMAGES
EXPECTATION DAMAGES
Expectation damages are damages to provide the non-breaching party with the exchange bargained for. Under Hadley-Baxendale, damages must be contemplated by the parties at the time of contract formation.

COVER PRICE
Here, the Owner bargained for a fully functional solar heating system for the price of $50,000. The value of the parking space that was to be provided, was established by the contract to be $15,000. As a result of the Contractor's breach, the solar system cost Owner $60,000. The value of the parking space is irrelevant for the calculation; therefore the difference between the contract price and the cover price was $10,000, which Owner can recover from Contractor.

LOST PROFITS
Generally, lost profits must be reasonably certain to be recoverable.

Here, this is a new establishment and profits would be very difficult to calculate. Therefore, lost profits resulting from the breach would likely not be recoverable and expectation damages will be limited to $10,000.

TAX REDUCTION

Under Hadley v. Baxendale the parties must contemplate damages at the time of contract formation. Here, though the contract stated that time was of the essence, the tax breaks were only instituted the day prior to the anticipatory repudiation. Neither party was aware of these yet-to-be-announced breaks; therefore they were not contemplated at the time of contract formation.

Therefore, the tax reduction will not be recoverable.

Therefore, in a breach of contract action, Owner will be able to recover $10,000 as a result of its increased cost to install system.

SON v. OWNER

THIRD-PARTY BENEFICIARY
See rule supra.

Son is an intended beneficiary of the Owner/Contractor contract where he is to receive use of 2 parking spaces for 5 years. He is specifically named and is intended to benefit. He is an intended beneficiary.

Son was a donee beneficiary as Contractor gratuitously conferred the benefit upon him. However, he has not materially changed his position in reliance upon this promise, and Owner will use the Contractor's breach as a defense, which relieves her of her duty to provide the space.

Therefore, Son will not prevail against owner on a breach of contract action for the failure to provide parking spaces.

RELIANCE DAMAGES
Reliance damages are damages that are incurred in anticipation of contract duty performance by the other party.

October 2016 California BAR EXAM with ANSWERS for 1st Year Law Students

ABOUT THE AUTHOR

Mary Therese Pardinek was born in 1958. As a child, she was precocious and boisterous, yet could not effectively function in many sports due to her excessive weight. She was over 100 pounds in the first grade. Instead, she spent many days and hours reading children stories popular in that era. Mary was especially attracted to stories where the hero had some deficiency, which became a benefit instead of a failing. She had to drop out of high school. However, she put herself through an accredited engineering program at Purdue University. Mary graduated from Purdue in 1984 with a bachelor of science in engineering, became an accomplished, and noted chemical and environmental engineer. Eventually, she ran and operated her own business. Now, retired, she writes and desires that her publications will inspire readers.

Attribution given to the State Bar of California for their permission to publish prior utilized CA Bar Exams with assessed high-grade answers. Thank you!

The State Bar of California Committee of Bar Examiners / Office of Admissions. 180 Howard Street • San Francisco, CA 94105-1639 • (415) 538-2300. 845 South Figueroa Street • Los Angeles, CA 90017-2515 • (213) 765-1500

www.ingramcontent.com/pod-product-compliance
Lightning Source LLC
Chambersburg PA
CBHW070312230526
45470CB00002B/835